Hiking in the Mountains
Is No Day at the Beach

Backpacking Life Lessons

•

by

Johnny Price

Published by Cotton & Cigars Publishing, LLC
Greenville, SC

Hiking in the Mountains Is No Day at the Beach
Copyright©2005 by Cotton & Cigars Publishing, LLC
ISBN: 0-9761982-1-5
Library of Congress: 2005933628

Cover art by David Wells

10   9   8   7   6   5   4   3   2   1

Acknowledgements

Many thanks…

First of all, to Bill Boswell, Chuck Cady, Travis Ellison, Travis Hooper, Darryl McElveen, Don Nichols, Andrew Shive, Jerry Shive and Steve Shive.

To Pam Scurry and Mimi Wyche for providing me with a safe haven and the encouragement to persevere.

To Sam Rhodes and Kathy Vass for their confidence and for being a team that makes things happen.

To Sandy Richardson, editor extraordinaire, who strenuously suggested I could be a better writer.

And to Emory Colvin, the tie breaker.

Dedicated to

Jerry Shive

Thanks, "Dad"

*An author is a fool who, not content with boring those
he lives with, insists on boring future generations.*
Charles de Montesquieu (1689 – 1755)

*Writing is not necessarily something to be ashamed of,
but do it in private and wash your hands afterwards.*
Robert Heinlein (1907 – 1988)

Your life would not make a good book. Don't even try.
Fran Lebowitz (1950 -)

*Life is Story
made to be told.
Since quill and papyrus
we've turned it to gold.
Handwashing optional.*
Johnny Price

Introduction

As a backpacker, I am a big time novice. If I ever go out by myself, I don't go far, and I don't stay long. I tend to be clumsy and inept. (Once I actually put my pack on upside down.) So when I was invited to take a trip out West with nine other men who, collectively, easily knew far more than I did about such efforts, I jumped at the opportunity—especially when the whole trip was planned, assembled, and executed by someone else!

> Tell me thy company, and I'll tell thee what thou art.
>
> **Cervantes**

From our departure through our return, the ten-day trip took place in early September. Three days were spent backpacking in Yellowstone National Park, the next day we rafted the Snake River just outside of Jackson Hole, Wyoming, and then we followed up with four days of hiking the Teton Crest Trail.

The planner, Jerry, did all the preparatory work: traveling dates, trail permits, meal plans. He ordered all the food, divided it up, packed it, assigned who would carry which meals, and then while on the trail, he did all the cooking. This was the third trip I'd taken with Jerry (the first two were to Alaska), and each time he did all the work. All I had to do was walk. I love Jerry.

Darryl, a veterinarian, entertained us with animal health care stories never meant to be published, so I won't repeat them here. He and I were together on the second trip to Alaska. Between that trip and this one, Darryl realized he could reduce the weight of his pack significantly if, instead of carrying his double-malt Scotch in its own bottle, he poured it into a plastic Nalgene bottle. He's a good man and happy to share his Scotch.

Don is one of Darryl's best friends. They were tent mates. At the end of a day's hike, these two could have their tent set up and be lying in it quicker than anyone I've ever seen. Don shared some really good cigars with us, and since I like really good cigars and don't believe there is such a thing as good double-malt Scotch, I like Don more than I like Darryl.

Steve bunked with me in my tent while in Yellowstone. He is a Presbyterian pastor from Grand Rapids, Michigan

> *The company of just and righteous men is better than wealth and a rich estate.*
> **Euripides**

who, because the nights were so cold, didn't want to climb out of the tent to do *anything*. He carried around a bright red, traveling urinal, and so I got a little nervous when I heard him rustling around at two in the morning.

Travis and I shared tents on those two Alaskan trips and on the Teton Crest Trail this trip. He's an M.D., admired for his patience, good humor, knowledge, and his willingness to stock plenty of drugs in his pack.

Bill would have been Travis' tent mate on the Teton Crest Trail, but he loves to fly fish and conspired to pull a groin muscle in Yellowstone, which required him to stay behind in Jackson Hole with rod and reel and waders rather than ascending to 10,000 plus feet behind the Grand Teton. He bequeathed his pair of really warm underwear to me.

Chuck, the librarian, is Jerry's brother-in-law. He's gone on every one of Jerry's "big trips," and he and I have taken a couple of side trips together in Alaska. Not surprisingly, he's a very well read, well-versed conversationalist—just the type you want out in the middle of nowhere with little else to do but think and talk, and talk about what you're thinking.

Young Travis serves as a model of courtesy and displays a constant willingness to go the extra mile to help others. Of course when I saw him drop his pack and *literally run* up a giant hill like Maria von Trapp *right after* we had reached the Teton Trail's summit, it was obvious he could handle a *number* of extra miles.

Finally, there was Andrew, Jerry's son and one of young Travis' best friends. They make a fun pair. Andrew likes to tell Travis what to do. Travis, in response, simply smiles back. Andrew has many of his dad's strengths. If over the years, he continues to develop those strengths I admire most, perhaps he'll invite me on some camping trips.

We may not have compared well to Tolkien's Bilbo Baggins and his fellowship, but these were my companions. We were off! … And, for me, some major life lessons came into focus.

Farewell we call to hearth and hall!
Though wind may blow and rain may fall,
We must away ere break of day
Far over wood and mountain tall.

Lord of the Rings

Chapter One

What? Me Worry?
~Alfred E. Neuman

Here's how it started: not well.

Saturday morning, we drove into Yellowstone to start our first day of hiking on the Specimen Creek Trail. Our plans called for a 27.5-mile loop hike and two nights of camping before exiting again at the parking lot.

Due to commitments prior to leaving home, I'd slept only two and a half hours before arriving at the airport at 4:00 Friday morning to catch a 6:00 flight from Greenville, South Carolina, into Jackson Hole, Wyoming.

So there I was, fatigued already.

Then it rained, and temperatures rose only just above fifty degrees, so it was a lot wet and a little chilly. That, combined with a 45-degree angle climb carrying a full pack, told my body it was no longer operating with the accustomed amount of oxygen. The decreased amount available at 8000 plus feet had me sucking air like an Oreck® vacuum cleaner. My legs ached. My right hip burned. My lungs hurt.

Had the trail recently been under much foot travel, our boots would have been simply sucking up mud. But as it was, we hiked over wet leaves and then more wet leaves that covered already slippery rocks. As we continued to climb, the rain fell, and the trail got slicker. All I could see was more altitude to conquer, and I was very aware that we had to cover eight more miles before we could make camp—and that this was only the *first* day.

Prior to leaving, I had caught a glimpse of the profile of the Teton Crest Trail, which gave me a side view of the terrain to be covered. Though not to scale, it gives the elevation gains so that by comparing those with the distances to be covered, you can more easily discern the difficulty. We were

> *It is a consolation to the wretched to have companions in misery.*
> **Publilius Syrus Maxim 995**

looking at climbing a total of 9500 feet, peaking at 10,050 feet above sea level before our trip would end.

Wet, cold, and tired, I was not happy. I was not confident. I didn't feel very grown up. But still, I thought I could make it, only not without a great deal of whimpering.

The silence of the others, broken by their heavy breathing and an occasional grunt, suggested perhaps some shared suffering.

Chapter Two

*Business is not just doing deals; business is having great
engineering and providing tremendous service to customers.
Finally, business is a cobweb of human relationships.*
~H. Ross Perot

When I'm out in the wilds, I bring a lot of stuff with
me: tent, sleeping bag, poncho, stove, water purifier. I bring
all this hoping to keep myself as comfortably miserable as
possible and trusting that the people who manufactured
the stuff did their very best work. I bring it along, grateful
for the folks who not only sold it to me, but that they also
made sure I knew how to work all of it.

Of course, it could work the other way, too. If
someone's slack on their job, I could break my leg in the
middle of nowhere when a trekking pole falls apart at the
edge of a cliff. It's the old adage: "For the loss of a nail, the
shoe was lost…for the loss of a shoe, the horse was lost…for
the loss of the horse, the rider was lost…for the loss of the
rider, the battle was lost."

Thankfully, I didn't have to worry about that. I had
some first-rate gear, my favorite stuff being my backpack,

my boots, my trekking poles, and my water bladder.

Whatever your hand finds to do, do it with all your might.
Solomon

My backpack design had two sets of adjustment straps that when pulled redistributed the weight more evenly on my hips, back, and shoulders. It's amazing the difference a couple of tugs can make.

Then there were my boots. In spite of all the hiking, I never had a problem with blisters. Jonathan Welsh, owner of Appalachian Outfitters in my hometown, ran me through a battery of tests before I bought my pair to make sure they were a perfect fit. Had they not been, he would simply have refused to sell them to me.

The world is moved along not only by the mighty shoves of its heroes, but also by the aggregate of the tiny pushes of each honest worker.
Helen Keller

As for trekking poles (which are basically a more substantial version of ski poles), they're like having an additional set of legs. And believe me, when I was ascending or descending steep inclines with loose rocks (especially in those rainy conditions) or crossing a rapid stream, I needed more legs.

Best of all was my beloved Camelbak® Water Bladder. (Officially, it's called an "Unbottle" but I like the word "bladder.") You fill that momma up with two liters of water, place it in a pocket on your pack, run the drinking tube up to your mouth, and suck on it all day long, never getting thirsty.

When I think about all the things I carried and how well they worked for me, I am grateful for the men and women who dreamed, designed, and developed my gear, fine tuning and improving it over time. Their work trickled down to provide me with reasons for confidence as I found myself transported into a foreign environment with a physical challenge that had proven in the first ten steps that it was going to be a hard one.

Backpacking Life Lesson #1

**We do not live, work or succeed in a social vacuum.
Our commitment to excellence at whatever we do
will very likely impact someone we'll never meet,
in some place we've never been,
in ways we'll never hear about.**

Chapter Three

So it is more useful to watch a man in times of peril,
and in adversity to discern what kind of man he is;
for then at last words of truth are drawn from the depths
of his heart, and the mask is torn off, reality remains.
Lucretius

As tough as the hike was for me, it was at times excruciating for Steve. This was his second such trip in two years. His first was a hike in Montana, followed by hip surgery and a slow recuperation that had put an additional fifteen pounds on his already hefty body.

As a youngster, Steve suffered from leg partheses, so that from the ages of six to nine, he couldn't walk on his left leg. It had to be pulled up behind him and strapped to his thigh, resulting in his left leg being about an inch shorter than the right. On top of that, he's got a couple of really bad feet.

Frequently on a steep climb, Steve would stop for a moment of recovery. I'd watch as he'd bend over, leaning on his trekking poles. Then he'd let out a short cry of low-grade anguish, grab the bill of his baseball cap, and squeeze out the sweat until it ran down his hands and arms.

Yet during the entire hike, Steve retained his good humor, never complained, never shirked his responsibilities. He persevered. The very fact that he was on the trail was an exhibition of great courage.

People who succeed in spite of circumstances that seem to work against them are ones to watch. It's more than just learning how to hike up a hill in pain, or paint pictures with our teeth when our arms won't move, or get out of bed in the morning when our hearts and minds give us not one reason to do so. We need to pay close attention to these folks because when their successes are accompanied by such things as good humor, generosity, graciousness, courage, and perseverance, we get insight into their character. That which surfaces as they live in and through one of these crucibles of life *is* character.

Occasionally we'll run into one of those rare individuals who, in addition to whatever problems they're successfully enduring, have such extraordinary character that they are willing to deliberately place themselves in positions of discomfort and risk for the sake of others, giving of themselves sacrificially, helping others with similar struggles succeed.

> *Character cannot be developed in ease and quiet. Only through experience of trial and suffering can the soul be strengthened, vision cleared, ambition inspired, and success achieved.*
> **Helen Keller**

Ironically, these very same people are frequently easily and casually dismissed out of hand. Their appearance, circumstances, and/or physical limitations immediately suggest to us that they do not meet certain standards that make us comfortable being around them or placing our confidence in them.

An even greater irony exists when those who succeed

> *We come from the creator, each of us trailing wisps of glory.*
>
> **Maya Angelou**

rather easily because of natural skill, good looks, and personality, often have few admirable character traits. You learn little from them beyond the mechanics of getting something done.

But those others—the ones who make it to the top of the hill, gradually perhaps, but who nevertheless are committed to accomplishing what is set before them because that is what they are there to do—*they* are the ones to observe, to talk with, to learn from, and to emulate.

Backpacking Life Lesson #2

Pay attention and learn from those for whom success is more difficult.

Chapter Four

You don't live in a world all alone.
Your brothers are here, too.
~Albert Schweitzer

When we started out in the pouring rain that first day, all the elements, including our rain gear, worked against us. The gear kept the rain out and kept us from getting cold, but with all the physical exertion, the insulation it provided was not enough to keep us from getting hot and sweaty. So while we weren't cold and soaked, we were hot and damp.

Four or five miles into the trek, we stopped for lunch and cooled down. Once we started back up the hill again, it was obvious that we had lingered longer than we should have because all of our muscles were tight. Water streamed down the trail, and Bill hit a bad spot on a descent, fell back, slid about six feet, and pulled his groin muscle.

He must have visited our druggist because I never heard him complain. We had covered the full 26 miles with 40 lb. packs in three days, and by that time, Bill was hurting big time, but I didn't even know he was injured until we got off the trail.

All in all, the final day in Yellowstone wasn't a bad hike, just ten miles with virtually no climbing. We were up early, out on the trail, and we made good progress. Right at the last stretch, Darryl spotted our van off in the distance and knew there was a cooler of cold beer inside. He began to sprint—full pack and all— toward the parking lot. The rest of us ran, walked, or limped as best we could, with no one worse for the wear—except for Bill.

Back in Jackson Hole, we had two nights at The Trapper Inn. That meant beds, hot showers, and a telephone (!). And the next day, we'd be rafting down the Snake River.

And what a river it is. As the chief tributary of the Columbia, it runs 1,038 miles, rising in Yellowstone National Park in the north-western part of Wyoming and then flowing

> *Security is mostly superstition. It does not exist in nature, nor do the children of men as a whole experience it. Avoiding danger is no safer in the long run than outright exposure. Life is either a daring adventure, or nothing.*
> **Helen Keller**

through Jackson Lake in Grand Teton National Park. From there, it turns south and west into Idaho and northwest to its junction with the Henry's Fork River. This, in turn, runs southwest, then northwest, crossing southern Idaho through the Snake River Plain where there are several notable falls. Following a bend into Oregon and a turn north, the river forms the Oregon-Idaho and Idaho-Washington line. It is near the Oregon-Idaho line that the

Snake's greatest gorge is found—Hell's Canyon. It is one of the deepest in the world, extending 125 miles (200 km) and reaching a maximum depth of 7,900 feet (2410 km.) The Snake then turns at Lewiston, Idaho, and flows generally west to join the Columbia River near Pasco, Washington. And we were going to enjoy three and a half miles of it.

But following that, I'd have to begin hiking the Teton Crest Trail. And I knew its profile. There was going to be a lot of climbing! So, as soon as I could reach the Trapper Inn, I made calls leaving everybody the same message: "You've got to pray me through the last four days. I'll be hiking the Teton Crest Trail, and I've seen its profile."

I was serious. I had no confidence in my ability to do well on the trek; the anticipation of the hike had become an actual burden.

There are burdens and there are **burdens**. And for me, this was a **burden.**

The Apostle Paul recognized that distinction in a letter recorded in the New Testament. In one breath he says, "Bear one another's burdens," and then in practically the next breath, he seems to contradict himself by saying, "Let each one bear his own burden." (Galatians 6:2, 5)

> *More things are wrought by prayer*
> *Than this world dreams of.*
> *Wherefore, let thy voice*
> *Rise like a fountain for me night*
> *and day.*
> **Alfred, Lord Tennyson**

We all have burdens. Some are our responsibility and ours alone. To expect anyone else on the trail to carry my pack would have been ludicrous, selfish, and demeaning. However, there are burdens that we unavoidably find ourselves under and we can't begin to lift them, much less carry them by ourselves. It is then that we need to be willing to call in the reinforcements of family and friends to help us shoulder the load. There is also the extra shoulder we need to be willing to provide for someone else when they need it. Sometimes there's not much we can do to help someone else. Sometimes the only thing we can do is pray, which I'm convinced is the **best** thing you can do at anytime.

At any rate, I was calling in reinforcements! After all, I knew the profile.

Backpacking Life Lesson #3

Have plenty of people know what you're doing and what you're up against. Then have them pray for you.

Chapter Five

Therefore do not worry about tomorrow, for tomorrow will worry about itself. Each day has enough trouble of its own.
~Jesus

That worry aside, the rafting was going to be a piece of cake. A bunch of men in one large raft, including a professional guide, would not require a great deal of effort on anyone's part. We'd hit some moderate white water, enough to get us wet, but no more risky than the log flume in an amusement park.

After a good night's sleep and a great breakfast of eggs, pancakes, bacon, sausage, orange juice, coffee at The Bunnery (gotta have the fuel!), we finally got started. We had bright sunshine, hardly any clouds, and the temperature wasn't expected to rise above 72 degrees. There was even a bit of a breeze. I had good company; we'd packed plenty of food and drink for lunch, and we planned to eat steak for dinner.

There's nothing more relaxing and soothing than floating down a broad, calm river. Bill and Don took a small boat out ahead of us in order to do some fishing, and we slowly passed them about an hour down the water. We pulled over to the side at one point so young Travis and Andrew could climb up a cliff and jump off a few times. Not generally being afraid of either water or heights, but being very uncomfortable combining the two, I stayed in the raft.

Then, it was back down the river in the raft. What little white water we ran into provided a welcome drenching of cold water.

> *You can never*
> *plan the future by*
> *the past.*
> **Edmund Burke**

Still, my thoughts kept moving ahead to the next day's hike. It was going to be tough. And the past three days in Yellowstone, as extraordinary as they were in many ways, had hurt. No one likes to find himself in a place that is excruciating, frustrating, unrelenting and inescapable, and that is what I feared The Teton Crest Trail would be for me.

But floating down that river gave me a chance to relax and put things in perspective. The previous three days were past. They had been difficult, but I had made it through. And it had been worth it. The next four days hadn't even started yet. And what I had right then was that day.

So it was time to make a choice:

- Did I live in the moment, enjoying and relishing the gift that it was?
- Or did I allow the present to be stolen from me by the frightening images in my imagination?

I decided to follow the wisdom of a Wise Man and let tomorrow take care of itself.

And, incidentally, I had a great day.

Backpacking Life Lesson #4

**Don't allow the difficulties of yesterday
to stir up anxieties about tomorrow
so that you're unable to enjoy today.**

Chapter Six

Our life is frittered away by detail...simplify, simplify.
~Thoreau

We got off the river, had our steak dinner, and the reality of what lay ahead returned with great clarity. In just a few hours, I'd be hiking that Teton Crest Trail. I had to do it. I was going to do it. And I really wanted to do it.

But what I *didn't* want to do and what I didn't *have* to do was carry any more weight in my pack than was absolutely necessary. Talk about carrying around extra burdens!

> *...let us lay aside every encumbrance and the sin that so easily entangles us and let us run with endurance the race that is set before us.*
> **Ancient letter to the Hebrews, New Testament**

It was time to simplify. I began un-packing and repacking my stuff.

The stuff I'd brought seemed like such a good idea when I first packed. There was a weather radio, but it wouldn't pick up a signal anyway, *three* books (now just *when* was I going to read three books?), and a hammock (?!). They were all outta there!

One change of underwear. That was all I needed.

I even yanked out that cardboard cylinder inside the roll of toilet paper. Who knew the difference an ounce of weight might make?

And I repacked the Big Red chewing gum that keeps me from getting so thirsty by reducing the jumbo seventeen-piece-pack to just two half-pieces per day. (I can make my gum last.)

I don't know how much lighter my pack became—maybe five pounds. But I know I felt more confident having taken the initiative to do what I could to change my circumstances. The rest of the worries were beyond my control.

Backpacking Life Lesson #5

Periodically take inventory of your life, discerning and ridding yourself of those extraneous things that are adding too much weight, too many burdens to your life.

Chapter Seven

Consider it all joy, my brethren, when you encounter various trials, knowing that the testing of your faith produces endurance. And let endurance have its perfect result that you may be perfect and complete, lacking in nothing.
~Saint James, New Testament

Just outside of Jackson Hole, the Teton Village Tram carried us 10,500 feet up to the point where we would enter Grand Teton National Park, a part of Bridger Teton National Forest. The first day was to be relatively easy, but the next three, well, you know....

We had scheduled a 5.9-mile hike to a campsite reserved at the North Fork Group site. We started out carrying full packs (mine being a bit lighter, of course). Steve's portion of the trip was over, so he and his urinal had returned to Grand Rapids, and Bill was still laid up with that pulled groin muscle. So that left eight of us.

Much to my surprise, I was actually feeling pretty good. Everybody, in fact, seemed to be feeling pretty good.

We moved along at a clip. The climbing wasn't so bad. My legs weren't aching. My lungs actually filled up when I

> *In everything worth having, even in every pleasure, there is a pint of pain or tedium that must be survived, so that the pleasure may revive and endure. The joy of battles comes after the first fear of death; the joy of reading Virgil comes after the bore of learning him; the glow of the seabather comes after the icy shock of the sea bath; and the success of the marriage comes after the failure of the honeymoon.*
>
> **G.K. Chesterton**

took a breath. The previous five days in the higher altitude, not to mention the hiking, had improved my wind. The aching and burning in my legs had made them stronger. And, of course, there were all those prayers I had requested.

We reached our campsite in practically no time. It was barely midday, and we still had plenty of energy, plenty of daylight. We didn't want to stop.

But there was a hitch. In the Grand Teton National Park, you can only camp at the designated site you've reserved. We knew the next site up the trail was spoken for already, as was the one after that. So Jerry pulled out the map. I didn't look.

He said our solution was just 3.3 miles ahead to where the trail took a short loop out of the park and into the Jedediah Smith Wilderness Area. In an area designated as wilderness, we could camp anywhere we were willing to pitch a tent.

So, we were off, and I was thrilled. I felt great. Every

mile we hiked and every hill we climbed that day was one less mile and one less hill we had to hike and climb the next. Those prayers I requested were being answered.

By late afternoon, we reached Fox Creek Pass. Off in the distance was a perfect view of the backside of the Grand Teton illumined by the setting sun. At that time of day in the Rockies, there is often a golden hue with a backdrop of blue that suggests that no other colors are ever really necessary.

I walked down to a stream to help fill water bottles, and then Travis and I pitched our tent. The good doctor with all his pharmaceuticals was now my tent mate.

Jerry began preparing dinner, and the others set up their

> *We cannot escape fear. We can only transform it into a companion that accompanies us on all our exciting adventures…Take a risk a day—one small or bold stroke that will make you feel great once you have done it.*
>
> **Susan Jeffers**

campsites. As I stood looking off at the glowing Grand Teton, I found myself completely engulfed with a contentment I had never experienced before and haven't had since.

We'd had a good day. We'd worked hard, but we'd had the resources we needed to accomplish what we set out to do.

We'd done it together. Although hiking is by its nature a very solitary experience, there is something about the presence and camaraderie of others along the trail that makes you, legitimately, wonder if you could have done it without them.

The day had been a perfect fit.

This contentment continued uninterrupted throughout the evening and into the night as I joined the rest around the campfire, ate pizza, smoked a couple of cigars, drank a bit of wine, talked, visited, and then settled down for the night outside our tent so that as I fell asleep— or awoke in the middle of the night—I'd be able to see the incalculable number of stars available in the cloudless and moonless sky.

Backpacking Life Lesson #6

The struggles of life serve a purpose that is greater than and goes far beyond any present difficulties.

Chapter 8

We had the sky, up there, all speckled with stars,
and we used to lay on our backs and look up at them,
and discuss about whether they was made,
or only just happened.
~Mark Twain, *Huckleberry Finn*

Extended time spent in wide, open spaces tends to raise big questions.

Here we are, a cluster of homo sapiens huddled together on a comparatively small blue planet somewhere in the middle of such vastness that, generally speaking, the best we can do is call it space.

What is all of that out there, out there for?

And there really is a whole lot out there. In fact, there's so much out there that it is, for all practical purposes, immeasurable and by any stretch of the imagination, incomprehensible.

Each of us is miniscule compared with the size of the earth, and our sun is 1,300,000 times larger than the earth, with solar flares that at times blast out flames 50,000 miles high.

As if that isn't big enough, consider the constellation Orion—particularly his left "shoulder." That's the location of the star Betelgeuse. It is 50,000,000 times larger than our sun. And what's more, Betelgeuse and our sun are just two stars of approximately 100 billion in our galaxy, the Milky Way, which is only *one* of an estimated *10 trillion* galaxies.

> *Two things fill the mind with ever-increasing wonder and awe, the more often and the more intensely the mind of thought is drawn to them: the starry heavens above me and the moral law within me.*
>
> **Immanuel Kant**

I remember reading that in July 2003, a team of astronomers from the Australian National University calculated that the total number of stars in the known universe is 70,000 million million million (that's 21 zeros, incidentally) or more accurately, 70 sextillion. It's also about ten times as many stars as grains of sand on all the world's beaches and deserts.

Dallas Willard in *The Divine Conspiracy* noted that in 1995 the Hubble Space Telescope gave us pictures of the Eagle Nebula, showing clouds of gas and microscopic dust reaching six trillion miles from top to bottom. Hundreds of stars were emerging here and there from it, hotter and larger than our sun. He cited Joan Beck's description of it from the November 26, 1996, edition of the *Los Angeles Daily News*: "Towering clouds of gases trillions of miles high, backlit by nuclear fires in newly forming stars, galaxies cart wheeling into collision and sending explosive shock waves boiling through millions of light years of time."

Whew!

So, what is all of that out there out there for? Well, I think I found the answer. All of that is out there for your benefit and mine.

I believe the Creator of the Universe so wants to stretch and sharpen our fascination with the universe that He, in effect, calls our attention to the heavens and says, "Watch this! Take in as much of this as you can. See the splendor and the brilliant magnificence, the grandeur and the glory! Be caught up, and let your heart and mind and imagination soar in the wonder and the awe of the cosmos."

> *I have…a terrible need…shall I say the word?…of religion. Then I go out at night and paint the stars.*
> **Vincent van Gogh**

And then, perhaps, we would begin to suspect that the One who created and stands behind and sustains such immeasurable, incomprehensible magnificence must, Himself, be all the more magnificent.

If indeed we have a God who intends to be known, who intends to be noticed, recognized, and acknowledged, who knows that we need to know Him – well, then He's off to a great start catching our attention—if we will just look up. And down. And around.

In North America alone there are more than 20,000 species of plants that are native or have been naturalized. And they represent only 7% of the world's total. There are about 1,230,000 living multi-cellular animals species formally described in the scientific literature. There are about 50,000 species of vertebrates (fish amphibians, reptiles, birds, mammals), of which the majority (28,000) are fish.

Such diverse and intriguing works of art and life forms so abundantly available for us to observe beyond asphalt, artificial lights, brick and mortar are indicative—simply indicative, never doing full justice—of the creative imagination of the Creator.

Yet we mere mortals have so surrounded ourselves with the things that *we've* manufactured, things giving evidence to *our* brilliance and creativity, that for many of us the heavens are blocked from view, thus drowning out the voices that declare God's glory, leaving our own voices the only ones we hear.

> *Earth's crammed with heaven,*
> *And every common bush afire with God;*
> *But only he who sees, takes off his shoes*
> *The rest sit round it and pluck blackberries.*
> **Elizabeth Barrett Browning**

We've covered so much of the earth and manicured so much of the land, that we've lost much of that powerful sense of the wildness of nature. And now, the Creator Himself seems tame, if present at all.

If the heavens tell us, in part, of the Creator's immensity and magnificence and grandeur, the land gives us a hint of his wildness.

And there's one more amazing thing. The coordinated, orderliness of it all: from the swirling of the galaxies to the swirling of electrons, neutrons and protons. Of course, this is why we refer to it as the Cosmos, rather than the Chaos.

Backpacking Life Lesson #7

If you never leave town so that you always have asphalt underneath you and brick and mortar surrounding you, and at night, artificial lights above you, you will never experience and appreciate the extravagance of creation.

Chapter Nine

Do not forget to entertain strangers, for by so doing,
some people have entertained angels without knowing it.
~Ancient letter to the Hebrews, New Testament

Our trail led us above the tree line, permitting us to see miles of trail ahead, as well as the miles and miles of ground we had already covered. Looking back, we could see the same solitary hiker we had passed on our first day on the Teton. Around midday, we found ourselves a small grove of trees where we could settle in for lunch, and soon, our fellow hiker caught up with us. He stopped to unload his pack just on the other side of the trail less than a hundred feet away. There he lingered.

He was a short, wiry sort of fellow with close-cut salt-and-pepper hair and a couple of day's growth of beard. We introduced ourselves and asked if he'd like to join us for a lunch of burritos. Gil, as he called himself, moved right

> *...it is a matter of realizing that whatever I do is going to nourish either selfishness or charity in me. There is no third category.*
> **Thomas Howard**

over to our side of the trail. After we finished eating, he lingered to visit, and when it was time to continue our hike, he hoisted his pack and joined us for the next three days.

Gil was an avid hiker from California, and each year he took a major solo excursion that led him into Yosemite to areas made famous by Ansel Adams' photography. This year, he had tackled the Tetons. He had stories to tell about people he'd met, bears he'd encountered, weather he'd endured.

The people were almost always nice, the bears never were, and the weather didn't care. It could both soothe you and kill you the same day. Gil was reminded of that the time he made an embarrassing mistake, embarrassing because it was typical of novices.

Starting out on a day hike with warm spring weather and no threat in the sky, Gil hiked the miles that took him above the tree line and down into a valley that has a weather system all its own. Then the temperatures dropped, and fog set in. Rain mixed with ice began to fall. This was weather he had neither dressed nor packed for.

Hypothermia sets in when a person's body temperature drops to subnormal levels. Having experienced this myself, I know how quickly you can begin to shiver and shake, lose strength, and go through a complete emotional overhaul. And this type of sudden change in weather is a recipe for hypothermia.

Had he been a novice, Gil might have continued on deeper into the valley, unaware of the stealth changes taking place in his system. As it was, he survived and was now with us.

> ***That best portion of a good man's life,***
> ***His little, nameless, unremembered acts***
> ***of kindness and love.***
> **William Wordsworth**

We also learned that Gil was a deeply committed humanitarian. For years, he had worked in crucial developmental positions within health care administration and had spent a substantial amount of time in Calcutta working with Mother Teresa, helping to care for the poorest of the world's poor. He had actually hugged Mother Theresa, and I had hugged him. Imagine!

Stories to tell, information to share, insight to offer. Not a bad trade-off for a couple of burritos.

Backpacking Life Lesson # 8

Make sure you always have extra food in your pack and room at the campfire in case someone comes along and needs a meal or just some company. You never know how they might enhance your life.

Chapter Ten

*The highest reward for a man's toil is not what he gets for it,
but what he becomes by it.*
~John Ruskin

The last day on the trail, we climbed to the foot of the Grand Teton (aptly named by the French). We reached our summit, climbing to 10,050 feet above sea level.

I hate to sound anti-climactic, but once you reach that point, the scenery isn't that much to talk about. The Teton is impressive, towering above you another 3000 feet. But other than that, it's all pretty much brown. There are no spectacular far-off vistas or acres of impressive foliage. This is one case where the thrill is clearly in the accomplishment, rather than the destination.

Then came our marvelous descent of 7810 feet. First, we could hear the sound of water, then see it cascading off in the distance and below. The trail consisted of a series of cut-backs (much like when you line up for a ride at Disney World). So we were descending, catching sight of one set of falls, moving up along side of it, leaving it behind, only to encounter another and another. In bright sunlight, the trail took us through the North Fork Cascade Canyon, with Hidden Falls, Broken Falls, Glacier Falls, and Bannock Falls, all cascading through the rocks, down the ravines, into the valleys; roaring, shining, glistening, thrilling.

Quite a scenario for the final stretch of our adventure.

By trail's end, we were tired, dirty, and satisfied. Off the trail, Bill met us with the van stocked with—cold beer. Perfect ending.

> *Whatever a man sows, that shall he also reap.*
> **Apostle Paul**

Our packs came off for the last time. We stretched and sat and drank and found out that Bill was feeling better, especially since he'd actually caught a few fish. Then we got up, stretched, peed in the bushes, and tried to delay having to cram everything and everybody into the van.

But finally, it was back to The Trapper Inn—with beds, hot showers, and a telephone. And I made some "thank you" calls.

The trip hadn't been easy, but I'd known from the outset that it would be a challenge. The two things I didn't know were what exactly the challenges would look like and what pay-offs there would be by accepting them.

Of course, the two most obvious physical challenges were walking and breathing, but they resulted in increased strength and stamina. Then there were the emotional and psychological challenges.

Hiking, eating, and sleeping in remote wilderness areas, populated by all the creatures who call the wild their home—removing myself dramatically from my comfort zone—took me on an emotional journey ranging from loneliness, homesickness, and insecurity to exhilaration, awe, and gratitude.

The payoffs of all this included being forced to face my fears, rely on those around me for support and encouragement, and draw strength from the acknowledgment of the continual, if at times indiscernible, intimate presence of God in my life.

> *Isn't it nice when God's with you? Wonder why He can't be with us all the time? Maybe because we wouldn't appreciate it when He was. Or maybe He's with us all the time and we just don't know it.*
> **Horton Foote**
> ***Trip to Bountiful***

Another immediate payoff was just being there—in the moment—absorbing the beauty and opulence, soaking in through as many senses as I could that one opportunity presented to me by the presence and magnitude of a grand creation.

I continue to profit from those insights. I tasted an almost inexplicable quality of life that surfaced and flowed deep within me and which continues to revisit me from time to time, enabling me to better savor just being alive in this world.

By the way, besides a sense of accomplishment from having withstood the challenges, there was another big payoff: Strutting down the streets in my "I'm-an-Outdoorsy-Kind-of-Guy" Wyoming t-shirts.

Backpacking Life Lesson #9

If you want to experience quality, it is not going to be easy. Opt for easy and you sacrifice quality.

Chapter Eleven

*You need to claim the events of your life
to make yourself yours.*
~Anne-Wilson Schaef

One of the most important elements of any experience is the memory of it. That can be quite a payoff, too. So now I'm able (when I'm willing) during my present struggles to look back and be encouraged by the memory of perseverance—those first two days were *horrible*. I am reminded also of the importance of friends who plan trips and hand out ibuprofen and pray prayers and the necessity of continual reliance on God in order to be and do what I am meant to be and do—no matter where I am, despite any set of circumstances.

So, was it all worth it?

Absolutely!

There were times in the middle of it all when I was fairly convinced that it wasn't. But I was wrong.

And there was one more hard-core life lesson I learned:

Backpacking Life Lesson # 10

Make sure you travel with people who love you and understand you well enough so that they don't get too upset when you emit an odd noise and they perceive an unpleasant change in the atmosphere.

Left-over Observations

Through the centuries so many wise thinkers have made so many great observations that add substance to the preceding pages. Even the few I'm aware of are too many to include in the main body of this book. Still, I don't want you to miss them.

So here they are … in no particular order … all suitable for pondering, on whatever trail you travel:

> *We do not ask for what useful purpose the birds do sing, for song is their pleasure since they were created for singing. Similarly, we ought not to ask why the human mind troubles to fathom the secrets of the heavens. … hidden in the heavens so rich, precisely in order that the human mind shall never be lacking in fresh nourishment.*
> **Johannes Kepler, Mysterium Cosmographicum**

*Learn to get in touch with the silence within yourself
and know that everything in this life has a purpose.*
Elisabeth Kubler-Ross

*Give us grace and strength to forbear and persevere.
… Give us courage and gaiety to the quiet mind,
spare to us our friends, soften to us our enemies.*
Robert Louis Stevenson

*Prosperity doth best discover vice, but adversity doth
best discover virtue.*
Francis Bacon

*We may affirm absolutely that nothing great in the
world has been accomplished without passion.*
Hegel

*Orare est laborare, laborare est orare
[To pray is to work, to work is to pray].*
Ancient motto of the Benedictine order

Here hills and vales, the woodland and the plain,
Here earth and water seem to strive again,
Not chaos-like together crush'd and bruis'd,
But, as the world, harmoniously confus'd:
Where order in variety we see,
And where, though all things differ, all agree.

Alexander Pope

Death plucks my ears and says, "Live – I am
coming."

Latin Poet

True happiness is of a retired nature, and an enemy
to pomp and noise; it arises, in the first place, from
the enjoyment of one's self; and, in the next, from
the friendship and conversation of a few select
companions.

Joseph Addison

Fire is the test of gold; adversity, of strong men.
Lucius Annaeus Seneca

Slow down and enjoy life. It's not only the scenery you miss by going too fast – you also miss the sense of where you are going and why.

Eddie Cantor

What lies behind us and what lies before us are tiny matters, compared to what lies within us.

Ralph Waldo Emerson

Time is the coin of your life. It is the only coin you have, and only you can determine how it will be spent. Be careful lest you let other people spend it for you.

Carl Sandburg

You're only here for a short visit. Don't hurry. Don't worry. And be sure to smell the flowers along the way.

Walter C. Hagen

Eliminate something superfluous from your life.
Break a habit. Do something that makes you feel
insecure.

Piero Ferrucci

Manifest plainness,
Embrace simplicity,
Reduce selfishness,
Have few desires.

Lao-tzu

Good company and good discourse are the very
sinews of virtue.

Izaak Walton

The cost of a thing is the amount of what I call life
which is required to be exchanged for it, immediately
or in the long run.

Henry David Thoreau

We are always doing something, talking, reading, listening to the radio, planning what next. The mind is kept naggingly busy on some easy, unimportant external thing all day.

Brenda Ueland

It was a high speech of Seneca (after the manner of the Stoics), that "The good things that belong to prosperity are to be wished, but the good things that belong to adversity are to be admired."

Francis Bacon

No act of kindness, no matter how small, is ever wasted.

Aesop, *The Lion and the Mouse*

I expect to pass through this world but once; any good thing therefore that I can do, or any kindness that I can show to any fellow creature, let me do it now; let me not defer or neglect it, for I shall not pass this way again.

Ettiene De Grellet

Sweet are the uses of adversity,
Which, like the toad, ugly and venomous,
Wears yet a precious jewel in his head;
William Shakespeare, *As You Like It*

The philosophy which is so important in each of us is
not a technical matter; it is more or less dumb sense
of what life honestly and deeply means. It is only
partly got from books; it is our individual way of just
seeing and feeling the total push and pressure of the
cosmos.

William James

Nobody sees a flower – really—it is so small and it
takes time – and to see takes time, like to have a
friend takes time.

Georgia O'Keefe

The spacious firmament on high,
With all the blue ethereal sky,
And spangled heavens, a shining frame,
Their great Original proclaim.

Joseph Addison

The burning of a little straw may hide the stars, but
the stars outlast the smoke.

Voltaire

The appearance of everything was altered; there
seemed to be, as it were, a calm, sweet cast, or
appearance of divine glory, in almost every thing.
God's excellency, his wisdom, his purity and love,
seemed to appear in every thing: in the sun, moon,
and stars; in the clouds and blue sky, in the grass,
flowers, trees; in the water, and all nature.

Jonathan Edwards

The heavens themselves, the planets, and this center
Observe degree, priority, and place,
Insisture, course, proportion, season, form,
Office, and custom, all in line of order.
William Shakespeare, *Troilus and Cressida*

The real man is at liberty to be his Creator's
creature. To be conformed with the Incarnate is to
have the right to be the man one really is.
Dietrich Bonhoeffer